HITCHENS
VS.
BLAIR

HITCHENS VS. BLAIR

BE IT RESOLVED RELIGION IS A FORCE FOR GOOD IN THE WORLD

THE MUNK DEBATES

EDITED BY RUDYARD GRIFFITHS

BLACK SWAN

TRANSWORLD PUBLISHERS
61-63 Uxbridge Road, London W5 5SA
A Random House Group Company
www.transworldbooks.co.uk

HITCHENS VS. BLAIR
A BLACK SWAN BOOK: 9780552777902

First published in Canada in 2011 by House of Anansi Press Ltd
First publication in Great Britain
Black Swan edition published 2011

A CIP catalogue record for this book
is available from the British Library.

Addresses for Random House Group Ltd companies outside the UK
can be found at: www.randomhouse.co.uk
The Random House Group Ltd Reg. No. 954009

The Random House Group Limited supports the Forest Stewardship Council®
(FSC®), the leading international forest certification organisation. All our titles
that are printed on Greenpeace approved FSC® certified paper carry the FSC®
logo. Our paper procurement policy can be found
atwww.randomhouse.co.uk/environment

Typeset in Bell MT
Printed in the UK by CPI Cox & Wyman, Reading, RG1 8EX.

2 4 6 8 10 9 7 5 3 1

CONTENTS

Be It Resolved Religion Is a Force for
Good in the World   1

Christopher Hitchens in conversation
with Noah Richler   55

Tony Blair in conversation with John Geiger   67

About the Debaters   75
About the Moderator   77
About the Munk Debates   79
Permissions   81

Be It Resolved Religion Is a Force for Good in the World

Pro: Tony Blair
Con: Christopher Hitchens

November 26, 2010
Toronto, Canada

THE MUNK DEBATE ON RELIGION

PETER MUNK: On behalf of the Aurea Foundation, and on behalf of the Munk Debates, I'd like to welcome you all. I've been here for all six debates, and this time the excitement seems to be noticeable beyond the hall and beyond the city.

When we had the idea of starting these debates we hoped for excitement. The idea behind it was to try to elevate the quality of discussion, the level of dialogue on important global issues amongst Canadians. There are many ways of doing that, of course, but there was no better way than a high-quality debate, involving issues of vital importance to all of us, and discussions by people who are superbly informed and highly qualified — people who have the expertise, the knowledge, and indeed the commitment to the very subject we want to bring to the fore. And, I must say, to the credit of everyone involved in tonight's debate we did succeed.

Debates, in contrast to a speech, are multi-dimensional. It is a whole different ball game for our venerable guests to have the courage to come here in front of a large number of people, to be given no more than five minutes to offer their prepared presentation, and then to be faced with somebody equally as smart as you are, equally as well-prepared as you are, equally as committed as you are, but determined to destroy your points. And now you're rattled, you're shaken up, but you've got to come back and you've got to say something. And it is that kind of stimulus, that kind of adrenalin, that gets the most out of you. Brilliant minds, even mediocre minds, operate better under stimulus. We all operate better if we have been challenged.

So, in that spirit, this debate will not disappoint. I think the subject is as relevant as any subject we could have chosen. As to the speakers, we simply could not have done better. As to their commitment to the topic, no one can doubt the commitment of the two parties.

Before I conclude I would like to welcome three people. The first person is Rudyard Griffiths, the co-organizer of the Munk Debates and a member of the Aurea Foundation Board. It was Rudyard's idea to have this debate, and he deserves unlimited credit for this very successful Munk program. A great idea coupled with great execution can change the world. Rudyard is a brilliant creator and a brilliant executioner. Tonight, he will be the moderator of this debate.

Next, I'm personally and truly honoured to welcome our two debaters. First, I'd like to welcome the Right

Honourable Tony Blair, former prime minister of the United Kingdom. I don't believe that another human being has had as much impact on the events of the world over the past twenty or thirty years. I could not tell you how honoured we were when he accepted a role in this debate. And we know how committed he is to the side he is going to argue.

Next, I'd like to welcome Christopher Hitchens. The world has known many skeptics, but very few skeptics of his calibre. I do believe that if anybody can stand up to Tony Blair's razor-sharp debating skills — honed and trained over two decades in the British Parliament — Christopher Hitchens will do it and can do it. In my opinion, Christopher also happens to be one of the greatest minds of our time. Thank you for being with us.

RUDYARD GRIFFITHS: Welcome to Toronto, Canada, for the Munk Debate on religion, in association with the British Broadcasting Corporation. I want to begin by welcoming the worldwide audience of the BBC — some 240 million people that will have access to this debate through the BBC World Service, BBC online news, and BBC World News. I also want to welcome the tens of thousands of people watching this debate live on munkdebates.com — it's terrific that they're part of this conversation too.

I also want to turn my attention to this hall, this spectacular hall, the lucky 2,700 people who are here in the flesh to listen to this debate. Let it be said that on this day, thanks to the generosity of Peter and Melanie

Munk, Canada, and its largest city, Toronto, are truly at the heart of the global conversation.

Now, the moment we have been waiting for. We have our motion before us: Be it resolved that religion is a force for good in the world. All we need is our debaters. Please welcome Mr. Tony Blair and Mr. Christopher Hitchens.

Tony Blair was the prime minister of the United Kingdom from 1997 to 2007. Among his many international roles today, he is the Quartet representative in the Middle East, working with the UN, the U.S., Russia, and the EU to secure a lasting peace in the region. After leaving politics, Mr. Blair converted to Catholicism, and he launched the Tony Blair Faith Foundation, a global initiative to promote respect and understanding among the world's major religions. Many of us have read his recent bestselling memoir, *A Journey: My Political Life*.

Christopher Hitchens is a British-born American author, journalist, and atheist. His regular *Vanity Fair* columns and his prolific speeches and essays are essential reading for anyone and everyone concerned about global affairs. Christopher has a number of bestselling books, too — *god Is Not Great: How Religion Poisons Everything*, and his recently published memoir, *Hitch-22*. Christopher was recently diagnosed with esophageal cancer, and as such we are doubly grateful that he and his family have joined us.

Before getting our debate under way, let me briefly run down how the debate will unfold. Each debater has been given seven minutes for their opening remarks, for and against the motion. Next, Mr. Hitchens and Mr. Blair will confront each other through two rounds of formal rebuttals. I'll also be taking some questions from audience members on the stage. Those questions will be asked directly to Mr. Blair and Mr. Hitchens. We'll also be asking questions on behalf of our online audience. The debate will conclude with short, five-minute closing statements and a second audience vote on the motion.

Before I call on our debaters for their opening statements, let's find out how the 2,700 people in this audience voted. Twenty-five percent of you voted in favour of the motion, fifty-five percent opposed, and fully twenty percent of you were undecided. Now, we also asked a second question. We asked you if you are open to changing your vote depending on what you hear during the debate. Let's have those numbers too, please. Wow — seventy-five percent of the audience, that's three quarters, could change their vote, depending on what they hear during the debate. We will poll the audience again at the end of our proceedings to find out which of these two debaters was able to win by swaying us with the power of their arguments.

Now, the time has come for introductory remarks. Christopher Hitchens, as we've agreed, you will begin first with your opening statement.

CHRISTOPHER HITCHENS: Thank you very much to the Munk family. You are great philanthropists for making this possible. I have a text, and it is from Cardinal

Newman.[1] Recently, Cardinal Newman was beatified, and he is on his way to canonization. He is a man whose *Apologia* [*Pro Vita Sua*] made many Anglicans reconsider their fealty and made many people join the Roman Catholic Church, and is considered, I think rightly, a great Christian thinker. The text reads, "The Catholic Church holds it better for the sun and moon to drop from heaven, for the earth to fail, and for all the many millions on it to die, in extremist agony, than that one soul, I will not say, will be lost, but should commit one venial sin, should tell one willful untruth, or should steal one farthing without excuse." You have to say it's beautifully phrased. But to me, what we have here is a distillation of precisely what is twisted and immoral in the faith mentality. That is essential fanaticism, its consideration of the human being as raw material and its fantasy of purity. Once you assume a creator and a plan, it makes humans objects in a cruel experiment whereby we are created sick and commanded to be well. I'll repeat that: *created sick and then ordered to be well.* And a celestial dictatorship is installed over us to supervise this, a kind of divine North Korea. Greedy and exigent. Greedy for uncritical praise from dawn till dusk, and swift to punish the original sins with which it so tenderly gifted us in the

---

[1] John Henry Cardinal Newman (1801–1890), originally an Anglican clergyman and a leader in the Oxford Movement, which advocated the reinstatement of Roman Catholic doctrines and rituals into the Church of England. He converted to Catholicism in 1845 and became a cardinal in 1879. The quotation that follows is from the *Apologia* (1864), "Position of My Mind Since 1845" (originally "General Answer to Mr. Kingsley").

very first place. However, let no one say there's no cure. Salvation is offered. Redemption, indeed, is offered at the low price of the surrender of your critical faculties.

Religion, it must be said, makes extraordinary claims. Though I would maintain that extraordinary claims require extraordinary evidence, rather daringly religion provides not even ordinary evidence for its extraordinary supernatural claims. Therefore, we might begin by asking — I'm asking my opponent as well as the audience — is it good for the world to appeal to our credulity and not to our skepticism? Is it good for the world to worship a deity that takes sides in wars and human affairs, and to appeal to our fear and to our guilt? Is it good to appeal to our terror of death? To preach guilt and shame about the sexual act and the sexual relationship — is this good for the world? Of asking yourself the while, are these really religious responsibilities, as I maintain they are, to terrify children with the image of hell and eternal punishment, not just for themselves, but for their parents and those they love? Perhaps worst of all, to consider women an inferior creation — is that good for the world? And can you name a religion that has not done that, to insist that we are created and not evolved in the face of all of the evidence?

Religion forces nice people to do unkind things and also makes intelligent people say stupid things. Handed a small baby for the first time is it your first reaction to think, *Beautiful, almost perfect. Now please hand me the sharp stone for its genitalia that I may do the work of the Lord.* No. As the great American physicist Steven Weinberg has very aptly put it, in the ordinary moral universe the good will do the best they can, the worst will do the worst they can, but if you want to make good people do wicked things, you'll need religion.

Now, I'm going to say why I think this is self-evident in our material world. Let me ask Tony Blair again, because he's here and because the place where he is seeking peace, in the Middle East, is the birthplace of monotheism, so you might think it was filled with refulgence and love and peace. Everyone in the civilized world has roughly agreed, including the majority of Arabs and Jews and the international community, that there should be enough room for two states, for two peoples in the same land. I think there is rough agreement on that. Why can't we get it? The UN can't get it, the U.S. can't get it, the Quartet can't get it, the PLO can't get it, the Israeli parliament can't get it. Why can't they get it? We can't get it because the parties of God have a veto on it and everybody knows that this is true. Because of the divine promises made about this territory, there will never be peace, there will never be compromise. There will instead be misery, shame, and tyranny, and people will kill each others' children for ancient books and caves and relics, and who is going to say that this is good for the world? And that's the argument made from the example nearest at hand.

Have you looked lately at the possibility of what will happen when messianic fanatics get hold of an apocalyptic weapon? Well, we're about to find out as the Islamic Republic of Iran and its Hezbollah [Party of God] allies are in a dress rehearsal for precisely this event. Have you looked lately at the revival of czarism in prime minister Vladimir Putin's Russia, where the black-cowled, black-coated leadership of Russian orthodoxy is draped over an increasingly xenophobic, tyrannical, expansionist, and aggressive regime? Have you looked lately at the [religious] teaching in Africa and the consequences of it, of a church that says AIDS may be wicked but not as wicked as condoms?

RUDYARD GRIFFITHS: Christopher, thank you for starting our debate. Mr. Blair, your opening remarks, please.

TONY BLAIR: First of all, let me say it's a real pleasure to be with you and to be back in Toronto. It's a particular privilege and honour to be with Christopher in this debate. I'm going to make seven points — it's a biblical number — in my seven minutes.

The first is this: it is undoubtedly true that people commit horrific acts of evil in the name of religion. It is also undoubtedly true that people do acts of extraordinary common good inspired by religion. Almost half of health care in Africa is delivered by faith-based organizations that are saving millions of lives. A quarter of worldwide HIV/AIDS care is provided by Catholic organizations. There is fantastic work being done by Muslim and Jewish relief organizations. There are thousands of religious organizations in Canada that care for the mentally ill or disabled or disadvantaged or destitute. And here in Toronto there is a shelter run by Covenant

House, a Christian charity for homeless youth in Canada. So the proposition that religion is unadulterated poison is unsustainable. It can be destructive. It can also create a deep well of compassion, and frequently does.

The second point is that people are inspired to do such good by what I would say is the true essence of faith, which is, along with the doctrine and ritual particular to each faith, a basic belief common to all faiths in serving and loving God through serving and loving your fellow human beings. As witnessed by the life and teaching of Jesus, one of love, selflessness, and sacrifice. It was Rabbi Hillel who was once famously challenged by someone who said they would convert to religion if he could recite the whole of the Torah standing on one leg. He stood on one leg and said, "Do unto others as you would have them do unto you. That is the Torah, the rest is commentary."[2] Other examples are Prophet Muhammad's teachings: saving one life is as if you are saving the whole of humanity; the Hindu search for selflessness; the Buddhist concepts of *karuna, mudita*, and *metta*,[3] which all subjugate selfish desires to care for others; the Sikh insistence specifically on respect for

---

[2] Hillel the Elder (fl. 30 BCE–10 CE) is regarded as one of the most important scholars and theologians in Judaism. His "Golden Rule" is commonly quoted as a variant of the following: "What is hateful to you, do not do to your neighbour. That is the whole Torah. The rest is commentary. Go and learn!"

[3] *Karuna, mudita*, and *metta*: respectively, compassion, sympathetic joy, and loving kindness. Together with *upekkha* (equanimity), they make up the four Brahma viharas, or divine qualities to which humans should aspire in their relationships with others.

others of another faith. That, in my view, is the true face of faith.

And the values derived from this essence offer many people a benign, positive, and progressive framework by which to live their daily lives, stimulating the impulse to do good, disciplining the propensity to be selfish and bad. And faith, defined in this way, is not simply faith as solace in times of need, though it can be, nor a relic of unthinking traditions; it is still less a piece of superstition or an explanation of biology. Instead, faith answers a profound spiritual yearning, something that we feel and sense instinctively. It is a spiritual presence — bigger and more important, more meaningful than just us alone — that has its own power separate from our power and that even as the world's marvels multiply, makes us kneel in humility, not swagger in pride. If faith is seen in this way, science and religion are not incompatible; they are destined to fight each other until eventually the cool reason of science extinguishes the fanatical flames of religion. Rather, science educates us as to how the physical world functions, and faith educates us as to the purpose to which such knowledge is put, the values that should guide its use, and the limits of what science and technology can do — not to make our lives materially richer, but rather richer in spirit.

And so, imagine indeed a world without religious faith — not just without places of worship, no prayer, no scripture — but no men or women who, because of their faith, dedicate their lives to others, showing forgiveness where otherwise they wouldn't, believing through their faith that even the weakest and most powerless have rights and they have a duty to defend them.

And yes, I agree that in a world without religion, the religious fanatics may be gone, but I ask you, would fanaticism be gone? And then realize that such an imagined vision of a world without religion is not, in fact, new. The twentieth century was a century scarred by visions that had precisely that imagining at their heart, and gave us Hitler, Stalin, and Pol Pot. In this vision, obedience to the will of God was for the weak. It was the will of man that should dominate.

So I do not deny for a moment that religion can be a force for evil. But I claim that where it is a force for evil, it is based essentially on a perversion of faith. And I assert that at least religion can also be a force for good, and where it is a force for good is true to what I believe is the essence of faith. And I say that a world without religious faith would be spiritually, morally, and emotionally diminished. So I know very well that you can point — and quite rightly, Christopher does — to examples of where people have used religion to do things that are terrible and that have made the world a worse place. But I ask you not to judge all people of religious faith by those people, any more than we would judge politics by bad politicians or indeed journalists by bad journalists. The question is — along with all the things that are wrong with religion — is there also something within it that helps the world to be better and people to do good? And I would submit that there is. Thank you.

RUDYARD GRIFFITHS: Well, Tony, your training in Parliament had you land right on the seven-minute mark. So Christopher, it's now your opportunity, in our first of two rebuttal rounds, to respond to Mr. Blair.

CHRISTOPHER HITCHENS: Now, in fairness, no one was arguing that religion should or will die out of the world. All I'm arguing is that it would be better if there was a great deal more by way of an outbreak of secularism. Logically, Tony is right. I would be slightly better off — not much, but slightly better off — being a Wahhabi Muslim,[4] or a Twelve Shia Muslim,[5] or a Jehovah's Witness,[6] than I am, wallowing as I do, in mere secularism. All I'm arguing, very seriously, is what we need is a great deal more of one and a great deal less of the other.

I knew that we'd be told about charity. And I take this very seriously, because we're the first generation of people who know what the cure for poverty really is: It's called the empowerment of women. If you give women some control over the rate at which they reproduce, if you take them off the animal cycle of reproduction to which nature and some religious doctrine condemns them, and then if you throw in a handful of seeds and

---

[4] Wahhabism, a branch of Sunni Islam named for its eighteenth-century exponent, Muhammad Ibn Abd al-Wahhab (1703–1792).

[5] Twelve-Imam Shi'ism, the largest branch of Shi'a Islam, named for its belief in twelve divinely appointed leaders known as the "Twelve Imams."

[6] Christian denomination that originated in the U.S. Bible Student movement of the late nineteenth century; the name "Jehovah's Witnesses" was adopted in 1931.

some credit, the floor of everything in that village — not just poverty but education, health, and optimism — will increase. It doesn't matter where you try it. Try it in Bangladesh, try it in Bolivia — it works. It works all of the time. Name me one religion that stands for the empowerment of women or ever has. Wherever you look in the world and you try to remove the shackles of ignorance and disease and stupidity from women, it is invariably the clerisy that stands in the way.

Furthermore, I would hope Catholic charities are doing a lot of work in Africa. If I was a member of a church that had preached that AIDS was not as bad as condoms, I'd be putting some conscience money into Africa, too. But it won't bring back the millions of people who've died wretched deaths because of that teaching, which still goes on. I'd like to hear a word of apology from the religious about that, if it was on offer. Otherwise I would be accused of judging them [religions] by the worst of them [practitioners of faith]. And this teaching isn't done, as Tony says so wrongly, in the name of religion. It's a direct precept practised, an enforceable discipline of religion. Is it not so, in this case? I think you'll find that it is. But if you're going to say, "All right, the Mormons will tell you the same. You may think it's a bit cracked to think that Joseph Smith found another Bible buried in upstate New York, but you should see our missionaries in action." I'm not impressed. I'd rather have no Mormons and their missionaries, quite honestly. And no Joseph Smith.[7] Do we grant to Hamas and Hezbollah — both of whom will tell you, and incessantly, "Look at our charitable work. Without us, *effendi,* the poor of Gaza, the poor of Lebanon, where would they be?" And they're right. They do a great deal of charitable work. It's nothing compared to the harm that they do, but it's a great deal of work all the same.

I'm also familiar with the teachings of the great Rabbi Hillel. I even know where he plagiarized the story I mentioned earlier. The injunction not to do to another what would be repulsive if done to yourself is found in the analects of Confucius, if you want to date it. But that truth is found in the heart of every person in this room. Everybody knows that much. We don't require divine permission to know right from wrong. We don't need tablets administered to us, ten at a time in tablet form on pain of death, to be able to have a moral argument. No, we have the reasoning and the moral suasion of Socrates and of our own abilities. We don't need dictatorship to tell us right from wrong.

RUDYARD GRIFFITHS: In the name of fairness and equity, Mr. Blair, I'm going to give you an additional twenty-five seconds for your first rebuttal.

---

[7] Joseph Smith Jr. (1805–1844), founder of the Church of Latter Day Saints. According to Smith, an angel appeared to him and directed him to an ancient text, engraved on golden plates, that had been buried in a hill near his hometown in upstate New York; Smith's translation of the text into English became the *Book of Mormon.*

TONY BLAIR: First of all, I don't think that because you can point to examples of prejudice in the name of religion, bigotry and prejudice and wrongdoing are wholly owned subsidiaries of religion. There are plenty of examples of prejudice against women, against gay people, against others that come from outside the world of religion.

And I am not making the claim that everything that the church has done in Africa is right, but let me tell you one thing that it did do, and it did it while I was prime minister of the U.K. The churches came together and formed a campaign for the cancellation of debt. They succeeded, and the first beneficiaries of the cancellation of debt were young girls in Africa who were able to go to school for the first time because they had free primary education. So I agree that not everything the church or the religious communities have done around the world is right, but I do at least accept that there are people doing great work day in and day out who are not prejudiced or bigoted, who are working with people who are afflicted by famine and disease and poverty, and they are inspired by their faith to do it. And, of course, you do not have to be a person of faith in order to do good work. I've never claimed that, and I would never claim that. I know many people who are not people of faith, but who do fantastic and decent work for their communities and for the world.

My claim is very simple. There are people who are inspired by their faith to do good. I think of people I met some time ago in South Africa — nuns who were looking after children who were born with HIV/AIDS. Now, these are people who are inspired by their faith, working and living alongside and caring for people. Is it possible for them to have done this good work without their religious faith? Of course, it's possible, but the fact is, faith is what motivated them. So what I say to you is, what we shouldn't do is end up in a situation where we say, "Right, we've got six hospices here and one suicide bomber there and how does it all equalize out?" That's not a very productive argument.

I thought one of the most interesting things that Christopher said is that we're not going to drive religion out of the world. And that is true — we're not. And I think that debate between people of faith and those who are secularists is good and right and healthy, and it's what we should be doing. I'm not claiming that everyone should congregate on my slate. I'm claiming one very simple thing: If we can't drive religion out of the world because many people of faith believe it and believe it very deeply, let's at least see how we make religion a force for good, how we encourage those people of faith who are trying to do good, and how we unite those against those who want to pervert religion and turn it into a badge of identity used in opposition to others.

So I'll finish by saying this: there are many situations where faith has caused harm. But there are many situations in which wrong has been done without religion playing any part in it at all. So let us not condemn all people of religious faith because of the bigotry or prejudice shown by some, and let us at least acknowledge that some good has come out of religion and that we should celebrate the good.

RUDYARD GRIFFITHS: Christopher, your second rebuttal, please.

CHRISTOPHER HITCHENS: Just to finish on the charity point, I once did a lot of work with a man called Sebastião Salgado. He is a great man, a great photographer, and he is the UNICEF ambassador working towards the eradication of polio. I went to Calcutta with him and elsewhere. He nearly got rid of polio; he nearly made it a disease of the past, a filthy memory. Because of so many religious groups in Bangalore, in Afghanistan, West Africa, and elsewhere, there were parents telling their children, "Don't take the drops. It's a conspiracy. It's against God. It's against God's design." By the way, that argument isn't terribly new. When smallpox was a scourge, Timothy Dwight, the great divine who was the president of Yale College, said taking lots of injections was an interference with God's design as well.

We need organizations like UNICEF to get major work done, and to alleviate poverty and misery and disease. And for me, my money will always go to organizations like Médecins sans frontières/Doctors Without Borders [MSF], Oxfam, and many others, who go out into the world and do good for their fellow creatures. They don't take the Bible along with them as people do all the time when they go to Haiti. People's money is being spent flat-out on proselytization. It's a function of the old missionary tradition, which went hand-in-hand with imperialism. They can call it "charity" if they want, but it doesn't stand a second look.

So that's the business of doing good, except perhaps to add that both Mr. Blair and I at different times gave a lot of our years to the Labour Party and to the labour movement, and that if the promise of religion was true, had been true, right up into the late nineteenth century in Great Britain or in North America — that good works are what's required and should be enough, and those who give charity should be honoured — those who receive it should be grateful — there would be no need for human and social and political action. We could rely on people being innately good, which we know we can't rely upon, and which I never suggested that we could or should.

So what now? Could religion sometimes be a good thing after all? That is now the proposition. What would religion have to do to get that far? Well, I think it would have to give up all supernatural claims. It would have to say, "No you are not to do this under the threat of the reward of heaven or the terror of punishment in hell. No, we can't offer you miracles." Find me the church that will say, "Forget all that." And what about faith healing? The church would have to give that up. It would have to give up the idea of an eternal, unalterable authority figure who was judge, jury, and executioner, against whom there could be no appeal and who wasn't finished with you even when you died. That's quite a lot for a religion to give up, don't you think? But who would not say, "We'd be better off without it?" If religion was what

Tony Blair would like it to be — an aspect of humanism, an aspect of compassion, an aspect of the realizations of human solidarity, the knowledge that we are in fact all bound up one with another, that we have responsibilities to one another — there is actually a sense of pleasure to be had in helping your fellow creature. I think that should be enough. Thank you.

RUDYARD GRIFFITHS: Tony, your final rebuttal, please.

TONY BLAIR: It all depends on what your experience of religious people has been. My experience of the people I was with last weekend in Africa — and that includes deeply religious people — is not actually that they're doing what they're doing because of their belief in heaven and hell. They're doing it for the love of their fellow human beings. And I think that's something very fine. What's more, they believe that this love for their fellow human being is bound up with their faith. It is absolutely true that they might decide to do good deeds irrespective of the fact that they have religious faith, but their faith leads to an impulse to do that good. And I don't recognize Christopher's description of the work that they do. In Sierra Leone, there are Christians and Muslims working together to deliver health care. That is an example of religion playing a positive role. They're working across the faith divide because they believe that their faith impels them to.

When we look back in history, yes, of course, there are plenty of examples of when religion has played a negative role. But religion has also played a positive role in history, too. For example, when religious reformers joined with secular reformers to bring about the abolition of slavery. And let's get away from this idea that religion created poverty. There are bad things that have happened in the world outside of religion. And when you look at the events of the twentieth century and you see the great scars of political ideology formed around views that had absolutely dramatically at their heart the eradication of religion — fascism and the communism of Stalin — then what I would say to you is, if you get rid of religion, you're not going to get rid of fanaticism and you're not going to get rid of the wrong in the world.

So the question is, how do we make sense of religion's vital part in the world today, since it is growing and not diminishing? And this is where there is an obligation on the people of faith to try and cross the faith divide with those of other faiths. That is the goal of my foundation. We have people of different religious faiths — we've actually got a program in which young people team up with other young people of different faiths, and work together in Africa on malaria. And here in Canada, we have a program that allows schools to use technology to link up kids of different faiths across the world. And here's the thing: when they start to talk about their faith, they don't actually talk in terms of heaven and hell and a God that's an executioner of those that do wrong. They talk in terms of their basic feeling, that love of God can be expressed best through love of neighbour and actions in furtherance of the compassion and help needed by others.

In 2007, religious organizations in the U.S. gave one and a half times the amount of aid that the U.S. government did. Not insignificant. So my point is very simple. You can list all of the faults of religion, just as you can list all of the faults of politicians, journalists, and those in any other profession. But the reason why people of faith try to do good is because their faith motivates them to do so, and that is genuinely the proper face of faith.

RUDYARD GRIFFITHS: Well, gentlemen, thank you for a terrific start to this debate. The time has now come to involve our online audience through questions that have been debated on our discussion boards and some live questions from those in attendance. Christopher, we're going to start with a question from a young woman who would like to address you personally.

AUDIENCE MEMBER: My question is in regards to globalization. This century, globalization will bring together, as never before, nations and people divided by wealth, geography, politics, and race. My question is, instead of fearing faith, why not embrace the shared values of the world's major religions as a way of uniting humankind?

CHRISTOPHER HITCHENS: Perfectly good question, but it seemed to be phrased as a call for a common humanism. I didn't hear anyone say, "Wouldn't it be better if everyone at least joins some church or other?" Not a bit. Common humanism is not made particularly easier by the practice of religion, and I'll tell you why: there's something about religion that is, very often in its original monotheistic, Judaistic form, actually an expression of exclusivism. "This is *our* God. This is a God who has made a covenant with *our* tribe." You'll find it all over the place. It isn't always as sectarian, as foundational, or as fundamentalist as Judaism was and sometimes still is. But it's not unknown.

I mean, it's always struck me as slightly absurd for there to be a special church for English people. It strikes me as positively sinister that Pope Benedict should want to restore the Catholic Church to the claim it used to make, which is that it is the one true church and that all other forms of Christianity are, as he still puts it, defective and inadequate. How this idea helps to build your future world of co-operation and understanding is not known to me.

If we were in the Balkans and you tell me what your religion is, I can tell you what your nationality is. You're not a Catholic. You know less about Loyola[8] than I do, but I know you're a Croat and I know you're a Croat nationalist. Religion — and in fact any form of faith because it is a surrender of reason — is a surrender of reason in favour of faith. It's a fantastic force multiplier, a tremendous intensifier of all things that are in fact divisive rather than inclusive, and that's why its history is so stained with blood — and not just with crimes against

---

[8] St. Ignatius Loyola (1491–1556), priest and theologian and founder of the Society of Jesus (the Jesuit order).

humanity, but with crimes against womanhood, crimes against reason and science, or attacks upon medicine and enlightenment. If you look at the way Christians love each other in the wars of religion in Lebanon or in the former Yugoslavia, you will see that there is no conceivable way you will achieve anything like your objective of a common humanism by calling on the supernatural, which is, I think, our only chance of . . . I won't call it salvation. Thank you.

RUDYARD GRIFFITHS: Now, Tony, someone has the inverse question for you. It would be a great opportunity for you to respond to Christopher at the same time.

AUDIENCE MEMBER: The question I'd like to ask you, Mr. Blair, is how do you argue that religion is a force for good in the world when the same faiths that bind peoples and groups also deepen divisions and exacerbate conflict?

TONY BLAIR: Let me give you one example: the peace process in Northern Ireland, where in the end people from Protestant and Catholic churches got together and the religious leaders of those two churches tried to bring about a situation where people reached out across the faith divide. So what I would say to you is let's just nail the myth that exclusivism is solely the prerogative of religion. I'm afraid this happens in many different walks of life. It's not what true religion is about. True religion is not about excluding somebody because they are different. True religion is about embracing someone who is different. That is why the concept of love of neighbour appears in every major religion.

Christopher is absolutely right, Confucius did indeed say something similar to Rabbi Hillel. Jesus said, "Love your neighbour as yourself." And after the death of the Prophet Muhammad, the religion of Islam was actually at the forefront of science, and it was at the forefront of introducing proper rights for women for the first time in that part of the world. Christopher says humanism is enough. And what I say to that is, for some people of faith, it isn't enough. They believe that there is indeed a different and higher power than humanity — and that is not about them thinking about heaven and hell in the old-fashioned sense of terrorizing people into religious submission. They think of it in terms of how you fulfill your purpose as a human being in the service of others. And so, when we say that could be done by humanism, yes it could. But the fact is, for many people it's driven by faith. And so, yes, it's true you can find examples of where religion has deepened the divide in countries in sub-Saharan Africa. You can also find examples of where religion has tried to overcome those divides by preaching what is the true message of religion, which is one of human compassion and love.

RUDYARD GRIFFITHS: Christopher, I'll let you respond to Tony's statement about Northern Ireland, and Iraq, a war that you supported and in which religion played an important role, arguably, in the success of rebuilding post-invasion Iraq.

CHRISTOPHER HITCHENS: I don't like to miss out on a chance to congratulate someone on being humorous, if only unintentionally, for it's very touching for Tony to say that he recently went to a meeting that bridged a religious divide in Northern Ireland. Well, where does the religious divide come from? Four hundred years and more people in my own country of birth have been killing each other's children based on what kind of Christian they were and sending each other's children, in rhetoric, to hell. They have been remaking Northern Ireland, the most remarkable place in Northern Europe for unemployment, for ignorance, for poverty, and for, I would say, stupidity too. And for them to say now, "Maybe we might consider bridging this gap," well, I should think so. But I don't see how they can bridge that gap, if they listened to the atheist community in Northern Ireland, which exists, and if they listened to the secular movement in Northern Ireland, which exists. I know many people who suffered dreadfully from membership in it, not excluding being pulled out of a car by a man in a balaclava and being asked, "Are you Catholic or Protestant?" He said, "I'm Jewish atheist, actually." [The man in the balaclava then said,] "What are you? Protestant Jewish atheist or Catholic Jewish atheist?" You laugh! You laugh, but it's not so funny when the Party of God has a gun in your ear at the same time. And that was in Britain, and still is to some extent, until recently.

[On to the situation in] Rwanda. Do I say that there would be no quarrel between Hutu and Tutsi people in Rwanda? Belgian colonialism made it worse, but there are no doubt innate ethnic differences, or there are felt to be in Rwanda. But the fact of the matter is, Rwanda is the most Christian country in Africa. In fact, by one account there are large numbers of people in relation to the numbers of churches; it's the most Christian country in the world. And for the Hutu power, genocide was actually preached from the pulpits of the Catholic Church. Many of the people we are still looking for, who were involved in that genocide, are hiding in the Vatican along with a number of other people who should be given up to international justice right away. So, since Tony seems to like religious people best when they're largely non-practising but basically faithful, I'll say it's not entirely the fault of religion that genocide happened in Rwanda, but when it's preached from the pulpit as it was in Northern Ireland and Rwanda, it does tend to make it much worse. Thank you.

RUDYARD GRIFFITHS: Tony, you were intimately involved in the search for peace in Northern Ireland. I assume you had a very different perspective of the role that faith played in the resolution of that conflict.

TONY BLAIR: Yes, and I do work in Rwanda now. First of all, I think it would be really bizarre to say that the conflict in Rwanda was the result of the Catholic Church. Rwanda is a perfect indicator of what I'm saying: You can put aside religion and still have the most terrible things happen. It was the worst genocide since the Holocaust. It was committed on a tribal basis. Yes, it's true there were members of the Catholic Church who behaved badly in Rwanda. There were also members of the Catholic Church and other religious denominations who stood up and protected and died alongside the people of Rwanda. And as for Northern Ireland, yes, it is divided along Protestant and Catholic lines, but the politics of the situation in Northern Ireland had to do with the relationship between Britain and Ireland going back many centuries.

So my point is very simple. Of course religion has played a role and sometimes a very bad role in these situations — but not only religion. And we wouldn't dream of condemning all of politics because politics have led to Hitler or Stalin, or indeed what has happened in Rwanda. So let us not condemn the whole of religion because there are examples of where religion has had a positive impact. And I think Rwanda and Northern Ireland are classic examples. Even the Middle East peace process is an example. Yes, I agree you can look at all the religious issues there. But let's not ignore the political issues either. Frankly, at the moment, I can tell you from first-hand experience, the reason we don't have an agreement between Palestinians and Israelis is not to do with the religious leaders on either side. It's a lot more to do with the political leaders, so it's my branch that has to take the blame for failing to come to an agreement.

Yes, of course, a lot of these conflicts have religious roots, but I think it's possible for religious leaders to play a positive part in trying to resolve those conflicts. In the end, it's for politics and religion to try and work out a way in which religion in a world of globalization can play a positive role rather than a negative role. And if we concentrated on getting people of different faiths working together, learning from each other, and living with each other, rather than trying to drive religion out, which is futile, I think it would be a more productive mission.

RUDYARD GRIFFITHS: Okay, let's take another question. Christopher, this is for you to start with: "America is one of the most religious countries in the world and also one of the most democratic and pluralistic, both now and arguably through much of its history. How do you explain that seeming paradox?"

CHRISTOPHER HITCHENS: The United States has a unique constitution that forbids the government to take sides in any religious matter or to sponsor the church or to adopt any form of faith itself. As a result, anyone who wants to practise their religion in America has to do it as a volunteer — it's what Alexis de Tocqueville wrote about so well in *Democracy in America* — ever since Thomas Jefferson wrote to the Danbury Baptist Association in Connecticut during his tenure as president, saying, "Rest assured that there will ever be a wall of separation between the church and the state in this country."[9] The maintenance of that wall, which people like me have to

---

[9] Jefferson's letter was written on January 1, 1802, in response to a letter from the Danbury Baptist Association. The Baptists, a religious minority in Connecticut, had argued that their liberties were unprotected by state legislation, and therefore that their religious privileges were enjoyed "as favours granted, and not as inalienable rights."

defend every day against those who want garbage taught in schools and pseudo-science in the name of Christ and other atrocities, is the guarantee of democracy. By the way, for a bonus, can anyone tell me who the Baptists of Danbury, Connecticut, thought was persecuting them?

AUDIENCE MEMBER: The Congregationalists.

CHRISTOPHER HITCHENS: The Congregationalists of Danbury, Connecticut. It doesn't seem to matter very much now, but it mattered then. Give those Congregationalists enough power, as they did have in Connecticut, and just see how unfurry they looked compared to how docile they behave now that we've disciplined them. Thank you.

RUDYARD GRIFFITHS: Well, Tony, let me come to you with that same question. Is it just a case of American exceptionalism, or is the balance between pluralism and faith that's been achieved in America something that you're either seeing in other parts of the world or a model that could be exported globally?

TONY BLAIR: I think that what most people want to see is a situation where people of faith are able to speak in the public sphere but are not able to dictate. And that is a reasonable balance that I think most people would accept. Fanaticism is not a wholly owned subsidiary of religion. It can happen outside of religion, too.

So the question is, how do we ensure that people who hold faith deeply, who believe in pluralist democracy are able to participate in society without being denigrated, but at the same time respect the fact that ultimately democracy is about the will of the people and the will of the people as a whole? I think that most people can get that balance right. We are very lucky, actually, in our countries, because we are in a situation where people of different faiths are free to practise their faith as they like. And that is, in my view, an absolutely fundamental part of democracy, and it's something people of religious faith have to be very clear about and stand up and do.

One of the reasons I think it's essentially important for people of religious faith to have people like Christopher challenge us and say, "Okay, this is how we see religion, now you get out there and tell us how it's different and where it isn't different, how you're going to make it so" — and I think that's a positive and good thing. All I ask is that people accept that people of faith have a right to speak in the public sphere and that sometimes we do it because we believe in what we're saying and we're not trying to subvert or change democracy. On the contrary, we simply want to be part of the democratic process, and our voice has a right to be heard alongside the voices of others.

RUDYARD GRIFFITHS: On our discussion board, many people have said that religion provides a sense of community in modern societies. We're immersed in a consumer culture more often than not, living alongside fellow citizens who are more self-directed than other-directed. What do you say about the community function of religion? Isn't that a valid public good of religious belief?

CHRISTOPHER HITCHENS: Absolutely, and I say good luck to it. The way I phrase it in my book is that I propose a pact with faith, with the faithful. I'll quote from the great Thomas Jefferson: "I don't mind if my neighbour believes in fifteen gods or in none. He neither by that breaks my leg or picks my pocket."[10] I would echo that and say that as long as you don't want your religion taught to my children in school, given a government subsidy, and imposed on me by violence, you are fine by me. I would prefer not even to know what it is you do in that church of yours. In fact, if you force it on my attention I will consider it a breach of that pact. Have your own bloody Christmas, that's all. Do your slaughtering, if possible, in an abattoir, and don't mutilate the genitals of your children. Because then I'm afraid it gets within the ambit of law.

Don't you think that's reasonably pluralistic and communitarian of me? I think it is. Why is it a vain hope on my part? Has this pact ever been honoured by the other side? Of course not. If I believed that there was a saviour or a prophet, who had been appointed or sent by a god who loved me and wanted the best for me, if I believed that and that I possessed the means of grace and the hope of glory, I think I might be happy. They say it's the way to happiness. Why doesn't it make the religious happy? Don't you think it's a perfectly decent question? Why doesn't it? Because they won't be happy until you

---

[10] Thomas Jefferson, *Notes on the State of Virginia* (1787): "But it does me no injury for my neighbour to say there are twenty gods, or no god. It neither picks my pocket nor breaks my leg."

believe it too. And why is that? Because that's what their holy books tell them. Now, I'm sorry, but enough with saying "in the name of religion." Do these texts say that until every knee bows in the name of Jesus there will be no happiness? Of course it's what these texts say. It isn't only a private belief. It is, and always has been, a threat to the idea of a peaceable community and very often, as now, a palpable one. So I think that's the underlying energy that powers the friendly disagreement between Tony and myself.

RUDYARD GRIFFITHS: There was a big discussion on our web site around the topic of religion and its role in the invasion of Iraq. And Mr. Blair, the question is for you, and it's in response to a statement you once made about the interplay of politics and religion that many people commented on. To quote you directly, "What faith can do is not tell you what is right but give you the strength to do it." The question being, what role did faith play in your most important decision as prime minister: the invasion of Iraq?

TONY BLAIR: We can nail this one pretty easily. It was not about religious faith. I sometimes say to people, the thing about religion and religious faith is that if you are a person of faith it's part of your character, it defines you in many ways as a human being. It doesn't provide the policy answers, I'm afraid. So as I used to say to people, you don't go into church and look heavenward and say to God, "Right, next year the minimum wage, is it

6 pounds 50, or 7 pounds even?" Unfortunately, he doesn't tell you the answer. And even on the major decisions that have to do with war and peace that I've taken, they were decisions based on policy, and so they should be. You may disagree with those decisions, but they were taken because I genuinely believed them to be right.

RUDYARD GRIFFITHS: So, Christopher, the natural follow-up question to you is, how did you square the circle — or maybe you didn't — between your support for the Iraq war and, let's say, then-president George W. Bush and his very public evocation of faith in terms of his rhetoric around the invasion?

CHRISTOPHER HITCHENS: I don't think you can point out any moment when George W. Bush said he was under divine order or had any divine warrant for the intervention in Iraq. In fact, I'm perfectly certain he didn't. He might not have minded giving the impression [that he said he was under divine order] — in fact, he wanted to give that impression about everything that he did. George W. Bush is someone who, after various experiments in faith, ended up in his wife Laura Bush's church, the most comfortable place for him to be. She was the one who said to him, "If you take another drink, you scumbag, I'm leaving and taking the kids." Joining his wife's church was his way of saying he found Jesus and gave up the bottle. I was in a Methodist school for many years myself, and like a good Methodist George W. Bush says, "I've done what I can with this argument and with this conflict. From now on, all is in God's hands." That's quite different, I think. It would have made him a perfectly good Muslim, as a matter of fact: a combination of fatalism with a slightly sinister feeling of being chosen. What's surely striking to those who observed the debate on what Tony Blair and I agree to call the "liberation of Iraq" is the unanimous opposition of every single Christian church to it, including the president's own and without doubt the prime minister's own. The Methodist Church of the United States adamantly opposed the liberation of Iraq, and the Vatican adamantly opposed the liberation of Iraq, as it had the liberation of Kuwait in 1991. It wasn't the first time that a sort of sickly, Christian passivity has been preached in the face of fascist dictatorship, and I was very surprised at the number of liberal Jews who took the same view about a regime that harboured genocidal thoughts towards them.

And if it comes to that, then I'm not the arbiter of what's rational in the mind of the religious thinker. Given the number of Muslims put to the sword by Saddam Hussein's regime, it's quite extraordinary to see the extent to which Muslim fundamentalists flocked to his defence. But I don't expect integrity or consistency from those quarters. Many feminists around the world will say they worked for years to bring down Saddam Hussein, and they are very proud of their solidarity with those comrades, those brothers and sisters; we're still in touch with them. We have nothing to apologize for. It's those who would have kept a cannibal and a Caligula and a professional sadist in power who have the explaining to do. Thank you.

RUDYARD GRIFFITHS: Well, I want to go to our two final questions, and I believe our first question is for Mr. Blair.

AUDIENCE MEMBER: My question pertains to something that came up earlier this evening. Religion on both sides often seems to be an obstacle to peace in the Middle East, and I was wondering what role you believe it can play in a positive manner in helping to bring peace between Israelis and Palestinians.

TONY BLAIR: Well, a few months ago I was in Jericho, and they took me up to visit the Mount of Temptation,[11] which is where I think they take all the politicians. And the Palestinian guide suddenly stopped at one point and he said, "This part of the world, Moses, Jesus, Muhammad. Why did they all have to come here?" And I said, "Well, supposing they hadn't. Would everything be fine?" The guide said, "Probably not."

But the religious leadership can play a part in the resolution. For example, I don't think you will get a resolution to the issue in Jerusalem, which is a sacred and holy city to all three Abrahamic faiths, unless people of faith are prepared to find common ground so that they are entitled to worship in the way that they wish. And it's correct that in both Israel and Palestine you see examples of religious fundamentalism — people espousing and doing extreme things as a result of their religion.

---

[11] The mountain where Jesus was tempted by Satan for the third and last time (Matthew 4:8–11), identified with this site as early as the twelfth century.

But I can also tell you that there are rabbis and people of the Muslim faith on the Palestinian side who are desperately trying to find common ground and ways of working together. And part of the reason I started my faith foundation is that the degree to which the situation in the Middle East is the result of religion or the result of politics can be argued forever. But one thing is absolutely clear: without those religious faiths playing a positive and constructive role, it's going to be very difficult to reach peace. So my view again, and I think this is one of the debates that underlies everything we've been saying this evening, is: if it is correct that you're not going to eliminate religion, and you're not going to drive religion out of the world, then let's work on how we can make those people of different faiths — even though they believe that their own faith is the path to salvation — work across the faith divide in order to produce respect, understanding, and tolerance. Because believe it or not, amongst all of the examples of prejudice and bigotry that Christopher quite rightly draws attention to, there are also examples of people of deep religious faith — Jewish, Muslim, and Christian — who are desperately trying to search for peace and, with the right political will supporting that, who would play a major part in achieving peace.

So I agree that religion has, to one degree, created these problems, but people of different religious faiths working together can also be an important part of resolving these problems, and that's what we should do and it's what we can do, and with respect to Jerusalem it is absolutely imperative that we do.

CHRISTOPHER HITCHENS: A visitor goes to the Western wall and sees a man tearing at his beard, banging his head against the wall, shoving messages into it, wailing and flailing, he watches in fascination. Then the visitor finally breaks and says, "Excuse me, I couldn't help but notice, you're being unusually devout in your addresses to the wall, to the divine. Do you mind if I ask you what you were praying for?" The man at the wall says, "I was praying that there should be peace, that there should be mutual love and respect between all the peoples in this area." "What do you think?" says the visitor. The man at the wall says, "Well, it's like talking to the wall."

There are people who think talking to walls is actually a form of divine worship. And it's another instance of the difference between Tony and myself. He uses his giveaway phrase in the name of religion rather than as a direct consequence of scriptural authority, which is what I mean when I talk about it. No one's going to deny that there are awards of real estate made in the Bible; by none other than Jehovah himself that land is promised to human primates over other human primates in response to a divine covenant. No, that can't be denied.

When David Ben-Gurion was prime minister of Israel, he still called it a secular state; he called in Yigael Yadin and Israel Finkelstein and other Israeli archaeologists and said, go out into the desert and dig up the title deeds to our state, you'll find our legitim. That was the instruction to the department of archaeology after they conquered Sinai and the West Bank. They went even further afield looking for some evidence Moses had ever been there. They didn't find any, because there has never been and there never will be any evidence. But you cannot say that the foundational cause, *casus belli*, in this region, the idea that God intervenes in real estate and territorial disputes, isn't inscribed in the text itself. Not only in the Jewish text, thanks to a foolish decision taken in the early Christian centuries, where it was decided not to dump the New Testament and to start again with the Nazarene story. Great Christian theologians like Marcion of Sinope[12] were in favour of doing that. Why do we want to bring the darkness and tyranny and terror and death and blood and cultism of the first books along with us? Surely we should start again. But no, we're saddling ourselves with all of that.

So this is a responsibility for the Christian world too, and need I add that there is no good Muslim who does not say that Allah told us that we can never give up an inch of Muslim land and that once our mosques are built there can be no retreat, it would be a betrayal, it would lead us straight to hell. In other words, yes, people from the three religions jibber and jabber, all of them. You're quite right, God awards land, it's just that you've got the wrong title. This is what I mean when I say that religion is a real danger to the survival of civilization, and that it makes this banal regional and national dispute, which, if reduced to its proportions, is a nothingness.

---

[12] Marcion of Sinope (fl. second century CE), one of the most controversial figures in the early history of Christianity. Although eventually excommunicated by the Church of Rome, he had a large and well-organized following that survived some centuries after its founding.

It makes that not just lethally insoluble, but is drawing in other contending parties who openly wish for an apocalyptic conclusion to it, as also bodied forth in the same scriptural text — in other words, that it will be the death of us all, the end of humanity, the end of the whole suffering veil of tears, which is what they secretly want. This is a failure of the parties of God, and it's not something that happens because people misinterpret the texts. It happens because they believe in them, that's the problem. Thank you.

RUDYARD GRIFFITHS: We have the perfect final question. It's from a student at the Munk School of Global Affairs.

AUDIENCE MEMBER: A big part of this issue is our inability to stand in one another's shoes, with an open mind, and to understand a different world view. In this regard, can each of you tell us which of your opponent's arguments is the most convincing? Thank you.

TONY BLAIR: Now, this definitely never happened in the House of Commons. I think that the most convincing argument — and it is the argument that people of faith have got to deal with — is actually the argument that Christopher has just made, which is that the harm that is done in the name of religion is intrinsically grounded in the scripture of religion. That is the single most difficult argument to defend. And since I've said it's a very difficult argument, I suppose I'd better give an answer to it. My answer to it is this: There is a debate about the degree to which individual parts of scripture, abstracted from their time, are used to justify a view. Or, as I tried to do in my opening statement, you ask, "What is the essence of that faith?" And what is the essence of scripture? And then what you realize is that for example, as a Muslim, if you believe that we should live our lives according to the beliefs that were held in the seventh century, then you will end up with some very extreme positions. But there are masses of Muslims who completely reject that as a view of Islam. And instead they say, the Prophet in the seventh century was somebody who brought order and stability to society. Even though many Muslims today would agree that we want equality for women, back then what the Prophet did was extraordinary for that time.

When you consider Christianity, of course you can point to issues that now seem very strange and outdated. But when you consider Christianity as a whole, ask yourself what it means, what draws people to it. What is it that made me, as a student, come to Christianity? It wasn't to do with some of the things that Christopher has been describing, and you know I understand that there are traditions within religion. I understand that. I accept that. I see how people read certain parts of scripture and draw conclusions from it. But that's not what it means to me, that's not the essence of it. The essence of it is, through the life of Jesus Christ, a life of love and selflessness and sacrifice, and that's what it means to me.

So I think it's most difficult for people of faith to explain scripture in a way that makes sense to people in

43

the modern world. And one of the initiatives that the Tony Blair Faith Foundation has begun recently is a dialogue called the Common Word, which is an initiative to bring Muslims and Christians together to find a common basis of co-operation and mutual respect through scripture.

So, yes, the argument that the harm that is done in the name of religion is intrinsically grounded in the scripture of religion is a difficult argument. It is the most difficult argument. But I also think that there is an answer to it, and one of the benefits of having a debate like this, and of having someone make that argument and assert that point of view as powerfully as Christopher has, forces people of faith to recognize that we have to take this argument on to make sure that what I've described as the essence of faith, which is serving God through the love of others, is indeed reflected not only in our actions, but in the doctrines and in the practice of our religion.

CHRISTOPHER HITCHENS: The remark that Tony made during this debate that I most agreed with — I hope that doesn't sound too minimal — was when he said that if religion were to disappear, things would by no means automatically be okay. And he phrased it better than that. But it would be what I regard as a necessary condition that would certainly not be a sufficient one. And anyway, religion won't disappear, but I do think that the hold of it in people's minds can be substantially broken and domesticated. He is quite right about that, of course. I hope I didn't seem at any point to have argued to the contrary. I come before you as a materialist, after all.

If we give up religion, we discover what we know already, whether we are religious or not, which is that we are somewhat imperfectly evolved primates on a very small planet in a very unimportant suburb of a solar system that is itself a negligible part of a very rapidly expanding and blowing apart cosmic phenomenon. These conclusions to me are a great deal more awe-inspiring than what's contained in any burning bush or horse that flies overnight to Jerusalem or any of that. It's a great deal more awe-inspiring, as is any look through the Hubble telescope at what our real nature and future really is. So he's quite right to say so, and I would have been entirely wrong if I had implied otherwise.

I think I could say a couple of things for religion myself. First is what I call the apotropaic. We all have it. The desire not to claim all of the credit: a certain kind of modesty, you could almost say humility. People will thank God when they are grateful for something, but there's no need to make this a religious thing. The Greeks had the concept of hubris as something to be avoided and criticized. But what the Greeks would also call the apotropaic — the view that not all the glory can be claimed by a lot of primates like ourselves — is a healthy reminder too.

Second, the sense that there is something beyond the material — or if not beyond it, not entirely consistent materially with it — is a very important matter. This is what you could call the numinous or the transcendent, or at its best, I suppose, the ecstatic. I wouldn't trust anyone in this hall who didn't know what I was talking about. We know what we mean by it when we think about certain kinds of music, or certainly the relationship or the coincidence, which is sometimes very powerful, between music and love. Landscape, and certain kinds of artistic and creative work that appear not to have been done entirely by hand. Without this we really would merely be primates. I think it's very important to appreciate the finesse of that, and religion has done a very good job of enshrining that in music and in architecture. Not so much in painting, in my opinion. I think it's very important that we learn to distinguish the numinous in this way.

I wrote a book about the Parthenon, which I'll mention briefly. I couldn't live without the Parthenon. I don't believe any civilized person could. If it were to be destroyed, it seems to me that you'd feel something much worse than the destruction of the First Temple,[13] but we've lost an enormous amount besides by way of our knowledge of symmetry and grace and harmony.

But I don't care about the cult of Pallas Athena [in Greek mythology], it's gone. As far as I know it's not to be missed. The mysteries have been demystified, the sacrifices — some of them human — that have been made to those gods are regrettable, but have been blotted out and forgotten. And Athenian imperialism is also a thing of the past. What remains is the fantastic beauty and

---

[13] The Temple of Solomon, extensively described in the Hebrew Bible and Old Testament. According to scripture, the temple was destroyed by the Babylonians near the end of the sixth century BCE.

the faith that built it. The question is how to keep the numinous, the transcendent, I'll go as far as the ecstatic, in art and in our own emotions and in our finer feelings, and to distinguish it precisely from superstition and the supernatural, which are designed to make us fearful and afraid and servile, and which sometimes succeed only too well. Thank you.

RUDYARD GRIFFITHS: We'll give Christopher a pause here, and go to Tony on the question that has been at the centre of this debate: the rigidity or flexibility of religious doctrine. Your church, the Catholic Church, has just made a reversal of sorts on its policy around the use of condoms. They are allowed explicitly and only for the prevention of HIV/AIDS infection. Is that reversal positive? Is that decision an expression of flexibility or a critique of the decades of rigidity before this reversal?

TONY BLAIR: Well, I welcome it, but I'm one of a billion lay Catholics. I think many Catholics have different views on a whole range of issues upon which there is teaching by the Church.

I want to pick up on something that Christopher said, because I thought his discussion of the transcendent was very interesting. For those of us with religious faith, we acknowledge and believe that there is a power higher and separate from human power, and in a way I can't accept what Christopher is saying, but I can accept there is something transcendent in the human experience, and something numinous and even ecstatic. You see, for me, the belief in a higher power and the fact that we should be obedient to the will of that power, and not simply our own will, does not put me in a position of servility. Servility is not the word I would use. I would use the word obligation, and it is of course absolutely true that when I can point to any of the acts that I say are inspired by religious faith, you can say, "Well, they can easily be inspired by humanism." But I think that for those of us that are of faith, and do believe that there is something more than human power, this does give you humility.

I have witnessed this myself. To refer to Northern Ireland again, I remember when I met some of the people who were the relatives of those who died in the Omagh bombing that occurred after the Good Friday agreement and was the worst terrorist attack in the history of Northern Ireland. I went to visit the relatives of the victims, and I remember a man who had lost his loved one in the bombing saying to me, "You know, I have prayed about this, and I want you to know that this terrible act should make you all the more determined to reach out and to not stop your quest for peace."

And it is true that he could have come to such an extraordinary and transcendent view of forgiveness and compassion without religious faith, but it was religious faith that led him to that state. And so we can't ignore the fact that for many of us religious faith is what shapes us. And it's not because we are servile, or base our religious faith on superstition or anything contrary to reason. Indeed, this is why I've never seen a contradiction between a belief in Darwinism and being someone who has religious faith.

Those who have religious faith genuinely believe that it impels us in a way that is different and more imperative than anything else in our lives. We wouldn't be true to ourselves unless we admitted that. So that doesn't mean that someone who is of no religious faith couldn't be just as good a person. And I do not claim for an instant that anybody who is religious is in some way a superior or better person than someone who isn't. But I do say that religion can and does give billions of people an impulse to be better people than they would otherwise be.

RUDYARD GRIFFITHS: I'm going to ask for your closing statements. Christopher, will you begin?

CHRISTOPHER HITCHENS: I think the way I might do it is by commenting on what Tony just said. Because he succeeded in doing what I had hoped I might get him to do earlier, which is to allow me to drive him back into the territory of metaphysics. We needed to get beyond questions such as "Are religious people good?" "Are they bad?" and "Does religion make people behave better or worse?" and so forth.

I'll give you an example. I mentioned earlier that Tony and I have both had an attachment to the labour and the socialist movement in our lifetimes. For a very long time, that movement had a challenger from the left, the communist movement, which has only been dead a very short time — and it hasn't died everywhere yet. The members of the communist movement believed communism had a much more comprehensive, courageous, and thorough answer to the problems created by capitalism and imperialism than the labour movement did, and they proposed a fighting solution. And if I were to point to the number of heroic people who believed in that, and the number of wonderful works of especially fiction, novels, and essays written by people who believed in it, you probably would mention one of your own, a Canadian, Norman Bethune. He was a heroic doctor who volunteered in China on the Communist side [during the Second Sino-Japanese War]. He did amazing work; he invented a form of battlefield blood transfusion. He is just one among many examples. It was the communists in many parts of Europe who barred the road to fascism in Spain and kept Madrid for years from falling to Franco, Hitler, and Mussolini.

Gandhi may take too much credit for the Indian independence movement, in my view, but no one would deny the tremendous role the Indian communists played in helping to break the hold of Great Britain on their country. In fact, some people find it embarrassing to concede this, but I don't, I'm a supporter of it myself. At least half of Nelson Mandela's party, the African National Congress [ANC], were members of the South African Communist Party [SACP] until quite recently, very probably including Mandela himself. There's no doubt about it.

There was real heroism and dignity and humanism to the communist movement, but we opposed it. We said, "No, it won't work." Why won't it work? Because it's not worth the sacrifice of freedom that it implies. It implies that great things can only be done if you'll place yourself under an infallible leadership, and once a decision has been made you are bound by it. You might conceivably notice where I'm going here. It's the reason many brilliant intellectuals left the communist movement. They left it very often for as high a reason of principle as they joined it in the first place. And the names of their books are legion and legendary. The best known is called *The God that Failed*.[14] When the history comes to be written, no one will be able to say that communism didn't represent some high points in human history. But I repeat, it wasn't worth the sacrifice of mental, intellectual, and moral freedom. And that was the purpose of my original set of questions on the metaphysical side.

Consider this carefully, ladies and gentlemen, brothers and sisters, and comrades and friends, are you willing, for the sake of certain elements of the numinous, to say that you give your allegiance to an ultimate redeemer? Perhaps for a great record of good works, as Tony proposed? Because you're not really religious if you don't believe that there is a divine supervision involved. You don't have to believe that it intervenes all of the time. If you don't believe that, you're already halfway out the door, you don't need me. But are you willing to pay the price of a permanent supervisor? Are you willing to pay the price of believing in things that are supernatural?

---

[14] Book of essays, published in 1949, by six prominent writers — Louis Fischer, André Gide, Arthur Koestler, Ignazio Silone, Stephen Spender, and Richard Wright — who discuss their conversion to and eventual rejection of communism.

Miracles? Afterlife? Angels? Most of all, are you willing to admit that human beings can be the interpreters of this divine faith? Because a religion means you have to follow someone who is your religious leader.

You can't, try as you may, follow Jesus of Nazareth. It can't be done. You'll have to follow his vicar on earth (his own claim, not mine), Pope Benedict XVI. You have to say, "This person has divine authority," and I maintain that what goes with it is too much of a sacrifice of the mental and intellectual freedom that is essential to us to be tolerated. And you gain everything by repudiating that and standing up to your own full height. And you gain much more than you will by pretending that you're a member of a flock or in any other way any kind of sheep. Thank you.

TONY BLAIR: When Christopher mentioned the Labour Party, I recalled a party member saying, after the Labour Party suffered our fourth election defeat in a row, "The people have now voted against us four times. What is wrong with them?" I would say that the example of communism shows that those who want to suppress freedom, and those who have a fanatic view of the way the world should work, are not confined to the sphere of religious thinking. It is there in many different walks of life. So the question for me as a Christian, with a belief in Jesus Christ, is not how that makes me subject to suppression and servitude, but, on the contrary, how that helps me find the best way of expressing the best of the human spirit.

It was Albert Einstein — Einstein, in fact, was not an atheist; he believed in a supreme being, although he did not necessarily subscribe to organized religion — who said that religion without science is blind. He also went on to say that science without religion is lame. And I would say that faith is not about certainty for me. It is in part a reflection of my own awareness of my own ignorance. And though life's processes can be explained by science, science cannot explain the meaning and purpose of life. And in that space, for me at least, lies not certainty in the scientific sense, but a belief that is clear and insistent and I would say rational — that there is a power higher than human power, and that higher power causes us to lead better lives in accordance with a will more important than our own. Not in order that we should be imprisoned by that superior will, but on the contrary, so that we can discipline and use our own will in furtherance of the things that represent the best in human beings and the best in humanity.

So I think that this evening has been fascinating, and it's a deeply important debate about the single most important issue of the twenty-first century. I don't think that the twenty-first century will be about fundamentalist political ideology. I accept that it could be about fundamentalist religious or cultural ideology, but the way to avoid that is for people of faith to stand up and debate those people who are of none. Even though it is true that there are those who, in the name of religion and indeed as a consequence of religion, will sometimes do horrific, bad, evil things that are in my view totally contrary to the true meaning of faith, we must also recognize that there are people with deeply held religious convictions, and that those convictions impel them to be part of that world of peaceful co-existence.

So I don't stand before you tonight and say that those of us of religious faith have always done right, since that is plainly wrong. But I do say that throughout human history there have been examples of people inspired by faith that have actually, rather than contributing to the suppression of humanity, contributed to its liberation — spiritually, emotionally, and even materially. And it is those people that I stand up for here with you tonight. Thank you.

SUMMARY: At evening's start, the pre-debate vote was 25 percent in favour of the resolution and 55 percent against, and 20 percent were undecided. The final vote showed a shift and a disappearance of the undecided voters, with 32 percent in favour of the resolution and 68 percent against.

CHRISTOPHER HITCHENS IN CONVERSATION WITH
NOAH RICHLER

NOAH RICHLER: It seems to me there's an essential distinction to be made between faith and religion that I don't think Tony Blair was ever making.

CHRISTOPHER HITCHENS: I think there is. I don't think someone is religious unless they have faith in what St. Paul calls the evidence of things not seen — in other words, the supernatural or supervising deity, presence, force, who requires and expects certain kinds of propitiation. If that's not in your mind, then I don't think you're really a religious person at all. I mean, you couldn't have told from anything Blair said that he was a Catholic. He didn't rise to any of my baits about the Vicar of Christ, none of that, and none of his liberation charity theology type of mush actually requires transubstantiation — the real presence of Christ in the Mass — or all of the things you have to believe if you are a Catholic.

NOAH RICHLER: Did you expect, when you published *god Is Not Great*, for defending it to become such a job? I've heard you referred to as the poster boy of atheism.

CHRISTOPHER HITCHENS: I hate that! But I don't ever get tired of it because it's the most interesting subject. It's the original subject, including the first written texts, really. Religion is what we had before we had philosophy and before we had cosmology and medical care and all kinds of things. You can't get tired of an argument that's that extensive.

NOAH RICHLER: I wonder if you become impatient with having to argue such abstracted ideas of faith — for instance, as happened during the debate, about the impulse to be good as if it was solely a religious quality — when, as you pointed out, so much that is inimical about religions lies in their differences.

CHRISTOPHER HITCHENS: Well, it can be a bit like punching air, as can dealing with the argument from charity. If in a seminar you were to argue that I've committed a well-known fallacy by not deriving my conclusions from my premises and I reply, "You don't know what you're on about, I've just given ten bucks to a homeless person," my answer wouldn't be accepted. But if you're a religious person it's a fantastic counter-argument. It's the special permission they expect to be granted to talk nonsense.

NOAH RICHLER: It was good to hear you make the feminist point that the shortcut to alleviating poverty is through elevating the status of women. Is that something you insist on?

CHRISTOPHER HITCHENS: Well, I do, because it doesn't take very long for a new Catholic, the fresh Catholic convert, to bring up either charity or the example of Mother Teresa, which is usually thought of as an automatic winning point. And this was odd, because I thought possibly Blair had read my little book on Mother Teresa, and it's in the argument over her that I've made the point most often, because her teachings and entire lifetime of work were exerted to make sure that women could not get hold of the means of family planning, so that the effect she had on prolonging and entrenching and deepening poverty and disease hugely outweighed any good she might have done if she'd ever spent the money she raised on charity — which, as it turns out, she did not do anyway. So I'm quite used to the Mother Teresa argument. And then you simply have to ask anyone if they know of a religion — and not just a monotheistic one — that does not, according to the texts, consider women to be an inferior creation.

NOAH RICHLER: Is what you describe as the "numinous," the "transcendent," or, in extreme cases, the "ecstatic," a necessary position you had to work out to find some way of accounting for the mysterious?

CHRISTOPHER HITCHENS: Yes, because what one has to avoid is certainty. The Socratic principle is that you're only educated to the extent that you understand how little you know. Ever since one first started discussing the existence of God in the dormitory at school, you would hear people saying sincerely, "Well, you know, there's got to be something more than just all this." Clearly such thinking does not come from nowhere, it comes from people lying awake and having perhaps strange thoughts they cannot deal with, or emotional experiences they hadn't been able to predict, or moments where you feel that there's something larger than yourself — of which love is a pretty good test.

We aren't a particularly rational species; we look for patterns and we find them much too easily. It's good that we look, but we're very afraid, easily scared, terrified of death, and often we are very stirred without quite knowing why. Some fairly banal examples, I suppose, are landscape and music in combination, or alone; love in combination with either of these; or perhaps looking at the vault of Heaven, as Hamlet would have put it — at the "fretted gold" of the sky at night. Cataclysmic events, great impressive storms, earthquakes — all of this makes one feel that actually we're not just primates on a rock, though in fact such phenomena are completely compatible with the view that we're primates on a rock. What I think would be nice is if people realized, for example, that a lot of devotional music is actually written by non-believers. I suppose Verdi is the best example. The effect that the Parthenon has on me is of the numinous and the transcendent, but it's not religion.

NOAH RICHLER: You must have taken part in a Passover seder some time.

CHRISTOPHER HITCHENS: Indeed.

NOAH RICHLER: I'm glad. I believe that everything in Jewish culture from humour to skepticism can be explained especially by the moment in this meal in which the rabbi or the person at the head of the table is obliged to answer the question, "Why is this night different from any other night?" and that he must do so until each of the four sons is convinced or their eyes are heavy with sleep. I've always been affected by this idea that an answer can be different according to needs. Is it a contradiction for me to be an atheist but also to feel that this is at least a good moment for understanding a culture?

CHRISTOPHER HITCHENS: Not at all, because I think the Jewish Seder is one of the most interesting survivals of the Hellenistic period in Jerusalem, when Jews, before the big restoration of orthodoxy by the Maccabees, were calling their sons Alexander, as a lot of them still do, and had adopted the Platonic symposium and would lie on couches. One of the questions of the night is, "Why do we recline?" They drink alcohol, they ask questions, and the young ones are supposed to take that leading role. It's all taken from the Greek — and it was bound to lead to dissent. There's no doubt that Judaism is much nearer to being philosophy than religion, or rather much nearer to that claim than Christianity or Islam are, and that it is attractive for that reason. Leo Strauss thought that the great Jewish philosopher Maimonides[15] wasn't a believer, but that he just dressed himself up in that way. So the great tragedy for me is the fact that Hellenistic Jewry was defeated. That's what's celebrated at Hanukkah, and that's why I hate Hanukkah. The Hellenistic influence was defeated, and the old sacrifices and circumcisions were brought back.

NOAH RICHLER: Well, everything I remember about Passover from the time I was a little kid were the philosophical points being made — the arguments, the commentary.

CHRISTOPHER HITCHENS: It's a good start. I've not only been to one or two, but we usually try and give one if we're not invited, just for the children.

NOAH RICHLER: In your memoir, *Hitch-22*, you describe how you learned from your brother Peter that you had a Jewish grandmother, a fact your mother Yvonne wanted kept secret and of which you and your father were unaware. Do you think you can be shaped by a story you don't know?

CHRISTOPHER HITCHENS: Well, it would depend on how much of a ton of bricks it was hitting you. If I'd had no interest at all in the question before that moment, I don't

---

[15] Moses ben-Maimon (1135–1204), known as Maimonides, philosopher and physician and one of the greatest rabbinical scholars of the Middle Ages.

really know. After all, a lot of people who are, if you like, however we want to put it, authentically a hundred percent Jewish — who've always known — seem to treat it not exactly as a matter of indifference, but very nearly, usually for liberal-ish reasons. But I'd always thought that Judaism was a great subject. I think part of having been a Marxist meant I could not help noticing how many thinkers and writers of the left were Jews. And I also used to find any hint of anti-Semitism absolutely repulsive. I took it personally, in the way that one does something obscene — perhaps because anti-Semitism is something so anti-intellectual and, in a horrible way, pseudo-intellectual. It's quasi-theoretical, a lot of it, and there's something completely tainted and hateful about it, which I hope I would have felt anyway. Someone like Martin [Amis], for example, certainly does without any skin in the game. I hate the idea one would be thinking with — what, one's blood, but the sentiment was there, and some of it may well have come from things I had overheard from my mum — I never call her Mum, why am I doing that? — from my mother when I was small. Maybe it stayed with me without my knowing, that could be. Or, in other words, perhaps it was something that, when I found out, in a strange way I had known all along.

NOAH RICHLER: Did you feel any responsibility, almost as a scientist would, to revise what you'd said or who you'd been in the light of what must have been, objectively, such an interesting revelation?

CHRISTOPHER HITCHENS: I did make haste to go and see my grandmother, who was still lucid then, and question her as far as I could about where we were from and what it had been like for her. That was fascinating, but all rather a conventional script, actually — Poland, millinery and dentistry, low-level-but-not-horrible prejudice, the pressure to change their name. They all assimilated quite fast, and there was minimal upkeep of the ritual — nothing very exciting, actually. It didn't change my attitude to the texts, and politically and ideologically, no, because almost all the great critics of religion have been Jewish. My attitude towards Zionism had always been — and I'm sure always would have been — that I very much doubt it to be the liberation of the Jewish people.

NOAH RICHLER: Do you consider anti-Semitism a religious phenomenon?

CHRISTOPHER HITCHENS: Yes, and this is where Tony Blair would make a point that I would agree with because he would say if you got rid of religion you still wouldn't get rid of anti-Semitism. I'm sure that's true, but the reason for its virulence is religious. As I say in my book, there were no Ukrainians at the crucifixion, there were no Armenians, there were no Druids. If the events as described took place at all — and I think that something like that probably did, that some charismatic rabbi was executed for blasphemy — then the Romans did it but it was the Jews who thought, "Here's another false claimant." They were the only ones who knew him, really, and they spat on him and turned away and for that they're not going to be forgiven. That's why it took the church until 1964 to stop saying that all Jews were personally responsible. And still, most of them, in their hearts, haven't really taken that back.

It's the same with the Muslims. The first people who meet Muhammad are the Jews, and at first some of them are excited, thinking maybe this is the Messiah. But he is not, they decide. Private time with the Prophet is something that every Muslim in the world would give their all for, really to meet him, and this privilege was granted to a group who turned their backs. And they still, most of them, haven't really in their hearts taken that back. It's not going to be forgotten. Blair, in a banal sense, would be right about this — without religion there would still be anti-Semitism, I'm sure, but its roots are definitely religious.

NOAH RICHLER: When did your love of speaking well begin?

CHRISTOPHER HITCHENS: It was partly when I was at school. I wasn't going to make a name for myself on a playing field, but I was not bad in the classroom. I was interested in current affairs and there was a debating society, and I thought, "I'd like to do that." At that time, also, I was prone to stutter, and I was small and quite shy and I developed a stammer. That was acutely embarrassing to me, and I thought I might cure it if I forced myself to speak in public. As a writer, I don't have musical capacity, but, in compensation, I am a good reader and I talk and I think better than I write. I remember when I was working for the *New Statesman*, my test of a good article was how strongly it made the case, was it a good polemic, would it strengthen the left, essentially. Anyway, we were at some dinner somewhere in north London and Simon Hoggart, who was working for the *Guardian* then, said to me, "Liked your piece in the *Statesman* this week," and I said, "Thank you." And he said, "But I thought it was a bit dry, it was a bit dull — good argument and everything, and you made your case very well, but . . ." And I bridled a little bit — well, quite a lot, in fact — and said, "What are you talking about?" And very mildly and disarmingly he said, "No-no-no. Just relax. It's so much more fun hearing you talk than reading you. Why don't you try and write more as you speak?" I couldn't forget what he said, and it's worked on me. And now, really, the pleasure of writing is as if to consider myself trying to write a letter to an intelligent or amusing friend.

NOAH RICHLER: What has your illness done for you, if I may put it that way?

CHRISTOPHER HITCHENS: Yes, you can. Well — and he's always misquoted about this, he was talking about something else completely — but as Dr. Johnson famously said of the death penalty, it concentrates your mind. It does do that. But then, I'd like to think, mine was fairly concentrated anyway. Mostly, the thoughts that it sparks are ones that I think people in their early sixties have in any case — you know, "Where did all the time go?" and "What have I done with my life?" — but these have been hugely alleviated for me by the number of people who have written to me to say, "Don't worry, you haven't. You did this or that for me. I'm here to prove it."

I really have had so much more than I expected, and certainly more than I deserve, but it's coincided with a very active period in my life, and a very satisfying one, and that's both a nice thought and a very bitter one because you think, "Well, I've got to the point I wanted to get to, and I could claim I've worked bloody hard to do it, and here I was looking forward to some good sixties." I really didn't want more than that — a decade, basically, of dividend. It's not that I would stop investing, but I'd, you know, cash out a bit. And now I'm not going to get that, I don't think — well, no, I'm not, because even if I do have them they won't be carefree years in any sense. At best, the sickness will always be at bay. So I won't get that, and of course this is exactly the period where my children are at their most intriguing, and so, yes, that's very bitter. To some extent, I can be jaunty on my own behalf, or phlegmatic, whatever you want to call it, and very occasionally a little bit more stoical than I feel — I can be those things, but not for them.

NOAH RICHLER: After the debate I heard one of your fans say, "Hitchens's mind is the best argument for God." His partner replied, "No, it's an argument for science."

CHRISTOPHER HITCHENS: Well, they're both wrong, I think.

TONY BLAIR IN CONVERSATION WITH JOHN GEIGER

JOHN GEIGER: I'm going to begin by asking you if there was any conversion moment, when you first became aware that you have a strong faith, a spiritual [dimension]?

TONY BLAIR: Well, I had a curious upbringing. My dad was a militant atheist, or is a militant atheist. My mum was sort of brought up in a religious family because she was a Protestant from Ireland but wasn't especially religious. I mean, I went to a church school when I was younger and imbibed a certain amount of religion then, but it was really in university that I got interested in religion and politics at the same time. I don't think as if it were one moment of conversion, but my spiritual journey really began then.

JOHN GEIGER: Does a moral hierarchy exist among religions to this day? Are some a greater force for good than others or are they essentially moral equivalents?

TONY BLAIR: My faith foundation works to bring about a greater respect and understanding between different faiths. We basically work with six popular religions in the world which are the three Abrahamic religions, [as well as] Hinduism, Buddhism, and Sikhism. And the question I'm often asked is, "Well, you're a Christian, you believe in salvation through Jesus Christ, so how can you really respect someone of a different faith, who believes in a different path to salvation?" And the answer is that even if I have my own belief, I can still respect, not just the right of the person to hold that different belief, but also respect that belief. And one of the things that's been really exciting to me in the work I've done with my foundation is to explore and study different religious faiths, study not just their history and tradition but their belief systems. I've not in any way diminished my own sense of my own faith but, yes, of course, I believe it is possible for people to find a different path, to have a different belief system, and for me to respect that completely.

JOHN GEIGER: In a highly globalized world where diversity of belief systems is very much in the mix, how can religion provide common values and a shared ethical foundation, or can it?

TONY BLAIR: I believe it can. I mean, first of all, I think the place of faith in the era of globalization is the single biggest issue of the twenty-first century. I mean, it's not an issue like climate change is an issue, for example, or the global economy in its present crisis. But in terms of how people live together, how we minimize the prospects of conflict and maximize the prospects of peace, the place of religion in our society today is essential. And basically what is happening is that, in the process of globalization, people are being pushed closer together; so are people of different faiths. Canada is a classic example; it's a melting pot of people of different faiths and races and nationalities, and we're all pushed together. The question in those circumstances is, does religion become a force for bad, pulling people apart because religion is seen as a badge of identity and opposition to others? Or is religion essentially seen as being about certain values that guide your life, and what is common to all the major religions is a belief in love of neighbour as yourself and actually in human solidarity and human compassion. So in that sense, I think religion could be, in an era of globalization, a civilizing force.

JOHN GEIGER: You write in your memoir that, and I quote, "I have always been more interested in religion than politics . . ." You don't really develop this thought in the book, however, and I suspect it will startle many people, given your success in politics. If this is the case, why did you not set out to become, say, the Archbishop of Canterbury, or the Cardinal-Archbishop of Westminster?

TONY BLAIR: I know, it's slightly strange, isn't it?

JOHN GEIGER: And I suspect it will startle many who will see you, and this is a compliment, as being very much a political animal, and if this is indeed the case, why didn't you set out to be the Archbishop of Canterbury, the Cardinal-Archbishop of Westminster? Why secular politics?

TONY BLAIR: I'm not a good enough person to assume that type of role. You know, I often say to people about this that I believe in the power of politics to change the world. And as you rightly say, I'm very much a political animal. If you ask me what I read most about, I read most about religion. It interests me enormously. On the other hand, I always used to say to people that God doesn't tell you the policy answers. That's in the realm of politics. In the end, your faith is part of what you are, it's part of what you carry, it's part of your belief system. It doesn't really, it can't, I'm afraid, write the white paper on education policy for you.

JOHN GEIGER: You attended Roman Catholic mass while you were prime minister but you didn't take that final step, conversion, acceptance into or being received into the Roman Catholic Church, until after you had left office. I wonder if this raises the inference that it would have been politically inexpedient for you to be a Roman Catholic prime minister, which itself raises questions about the limits of religious tolerance, of religious affiliation, even today in a country like the United Kingdom which is obviously a highly secular country despite the establishment of the church.

TONY BLAIR: It wasn't that it would be deeply controversial at all. Look, I never made any secret of the fact I went to mass, and my wife's a Catholic, my kids were brought up Catholics and went to a Catholic school. I wasn't, for reasons of religious controversy, not doing it. It's just, to be absolutely blunt about it — and I'm simply being honest with people about it — I had so many things, issues I was dealing with, I didn't really want to put that one on the table at the same time, because I just knew I would have endless explanations to make and conspiracy theories about why I decided to do it and all sorts of stuff written about what I believed about the establishment of the Church of England and so on. So really, I mean this may reflect to my discredit, I don't know, but I just literally decided it was something I didn't want to have as an additional issue alongside all the other issues I had. But, you know, I've been attending mass for twenty-five years, and it was a completely logical step for me to be able to take communion in a Catholic church along with my family.

JOHN GEIGER: Is there someone in politics, someone you've known who best exemplifies faith [in] public service, someone you've looked to as an example or inspiration?

TONY BLAIR: I don't know, really. Faith plays a far greater role in political leaders than you might think, actually. And it's interesting when I have talked to other leaders about faith, some of them you wouldn't have thought were people with a religious conviction at all, but turned out to have. I don't know that I would pull one figure out, actually. I mean, I was going to talk about Gandhi, but then on the other hand it's always unclear as to exactly what role religion played in his political life. No, I think there are lots of leaders I admire, but I don't think there's someone I would pick out particularly for religious conviction.

JOHN GEIGER: You mentioned you do a lot of reading of religious materials. Is there something that you would fall back on as being central to your thinking?

TONY BLAIR: There's nothing I would say that I've read that has kind of changed my entire perception, but there's a lot that I have read that has been a fascination and education to me. So, you know, there is a wonderful set of books about Islam, which have been very interesting to me. There's a book I've read recently that was written about the Prophet Muhammad, but based on all the contemporary sources about him, which is a very interesting book. Rowan Williams, who's Archbishop of Canterbury, wrote a biography of Arius.[16] It's the Arian heresy that gave rise to all the controversies of the fourth century. It's a fascinating book to read.

So I tend to read more because I'm interested in knowing, I'm interested in knowing about scripture. I read books that are a lot about the history of the church and

---

[16] Arius (ca. 250–336), a scholar whose teachings about the relationship of God the Father to God the Son (a subject that had already been debated for many years) came to the fore in the early fourth century. The resulting controversy led to the convening of the First Council of Nicea by the Emperor Constantine in 325. Williams's book *Arius: Heresy and Tradition* was originally published in 1987.

the history of religion. Karen Armstrong's written some wonderful books about religion.

JOHN GEIGER: I'll just have one last question and that is, the concept of redemption is part of the essence of Christianity. What is it that you seek redemption for — is it something in your own life that you believe that you . . .

TONY BLAIR: There's no sort of particular thing that I would pick out, but I think that one of the things that I think religious faiths do, or should do for you, is to have some sense of humility about yourself, your own failings, your own shortcomings. Now, it's perfectly possible to have that without religious faith, obviously, but I think it is the one of the disciplines religious faith imposes on you. So redemption, I don't think about something specific when I think of that, but I think about the degree of which I fall short from the best that I could be, which I guess is the same for most of us.

And you know, to say something about the foundation, which is operating now, we have a university program which McGill is a part of, and then I've got this schools program — there are many Canadian schools that are now joining up to this. You know, I think, as I say, this issue of religious ideology is the defining issue of the twenty-first century. And I would say that even if you're not the slightest bit religious you can't really understand the modern world unless you know something about the faith community. And the great prediction that was made when I was growing up and at university — that as society developed, so religion would fall away — has proven to be one of the many wrong predictions that were made. The truth is, religious belief is still very much with us and very alive. And how we analyze its importance, and how we understand it and are educated about it, is a big challenge.

JOHN GEIGER: Well, thank you very much for your time.

TONY BLAIR: My pleasure.

ABOUT THE DEBATERS

CHRISTOPHER HITCHENS is a journalist and the author of twenty books, including the international bestselling book *god Is Not Great: How Religion Poisons Everything.* He is a regular contributor to *Vanity Fair*, *Atlantic Monthly*, and *Slate*. His writing has also appeared in the *Weekly Standard*, the *National Review*, and *The Independent*, and he has made television appearances on *The Daily Show*, *Charlie Rose*, and *Real Time* with Bill Maher. He was named one of the world's "Top 100 Public Intellectuals" by *Foreign Policy* and Britain's *Prospect*. His most recent book is the memoir *Hitch-22*. Christopher Hitchens lives in Washington, D.C.

TONY BLAIR was prime minister of the United Kingdom from 1997 to 2007. Since leaving office, he has served as the Quartet representative to the Middle East, representing the U.S., the UN, Russia, and the EU. In 2008 he launched the Tony Blair Faith Foundation, which promotes respect and understanding among the major religions. He is also the founder of the Africa Governance Initiative, an organization that works with leaders and their governments on policy delivery and on attracting sustainable investment in Rwanda, Sierra Leone, and Liberia. Tony Blair lives in the United Kingdom.

ABOUT THE MODERATOR

RUDYARD GRIFFITHS is a co-host of the Business News Network television show *SqueezePlay* and a columnist for the *National Post*. He is the co-director of the Munk Debates and the Salon Speakers Series. He is a co-founder of the Historica-Dominion Institute, Canada's largest history and civics NGO. In 2006, he was named one of Canada's "Top 40 under 40" by the *Globe and Mail*. He is the editor of twelve books on history, politics, and international affairs, and the author of *Who We Are: A Citizen's Manifesto*, which was a *Globe and Mail* Best Book of 2009 and a finalist for the Shaughnessy Cohen Prize for Political Writing. He lives in Toronto.

ABOUT THE MUNK DEBATES

The Munk Debates are Canada's premier public policy event. Held semi-annually, the debates provide leading thinkers with a global forum to discuss the major public policy issues facing the world and Canada. Each event takes place in Toronto in front of a live audience, and the proceedings are covered by domestic and international media. Participants in recent Munk Debates include Robert Bell, Tony Blair, John Bolton, Paul Collier, Howard Dean, Hernando de Soto, Gareth Evans, Mia Farrow, Niall Ferguson, William Frist, David Gratzer, Rick Hillier, Christopher Hitchens, Richard Holbrooke, Charles Krauthammer, Lord Nigel Lawson, Stephen Lewis, Bjørn Lomborg, Elizabeth May, George Monbiot, Dambisa Moyo, and Samantha Power. The Munk Debates are a project of the Aurea Foundation; a charitable organization established in 2006 by philanthropists Peter and Melanie Munk to promote public policy research and discussion. For more information visit www.munkdebates.com.

PERMISSIONS

Also available

The Munk Debates: Volume One
Edited by Rudyard Griffiths
Introduction by Peter Munk

ISBN 978-0-88784-248-1

Launched in 2008 by philanthropists Peter and Melanie Munk, the Munk Debates is Canada's premier international debate series, a highly anticipated cultural event that brings together the world's brightest minds.

This volume includes the first five debates in the series, and features twenty leading thinkers and doers arguing for or against provocative resolutions that address pressing public policy concerns, such as the future of global security, the implications of humanitarian intervention, the effectiveness of foreign aid, the threat of climate change, and the state of health care in Canada and the U.S.

Intelligent, informative and entertaining, *The Munk Debates* is a feast of ideas that captures the prevailing moods, clashing opinions, and most imperative issues of our time.

Available in fine bookstores and at www.anansi.ca.
Also available as an e-book